Published by
Tutor Master Services

David Malindine

B.A.(Hons), M.A.(London), P.G.C.E.,
Adv.Dip.Ed.(Open), R.S.A. Cert.

Tutor Master Services
61 Ashness Gardens
Greenford
Middlesex
UB6 0RW

david@tutormaster-services.co.uk
www.tutormaster-services.co.uk

CW00494047

Acknowledgements

Thanks to Christine Malindine for preparing this book
and to Martyn Clarke for proofreading the scripts

For

Joshua and Frank

First Published 2015

© David Malindine 2015

ISBN: 978-0-9555909-7-9

Printed by G.H.Smith & Son, Design Printing Publishing, Easingwold, York

Tel: 01347 821329 Fax: 01347 822576

Web: www.ghsmith.com

Contents

Who this book is for

The ability to read and make meaning from written information are crucial skills for students of all ages. These skills are tested regularly in state, grammar and independent/private schools.

When children move from primary school to secondary school at the end of Year 6 aged 11 years, some parents may wish their child to take examinations in order to achieve a place at a grammar or independent/private school. Because the entry requirements to such schools vary from place to place around the country it is important for parents to prepare themselves by doing some research about the schools that they may wish their child to attend.

Schools publish their entry requirements for students moving schools at age 11+ and it is important that parents find out about the admissions policies of the school and any examinations that the school may set in order that they can prepare their children properly.

Examinations in English tend to be a reading passage accompanied by either a multiple choice or standard answer comprehension test, plus a piece of written creative writing, composition or essay.

For multiple choice answer tests, answers are recorded by ticking or marking a box on an answer sheet. For standard comprehension tests answers are written in an answer book.

It is my experience as a tutor that many parents enter children for more than one type of school. The Tutor Master papers take this into account by providing separate books with practice tests for both Multiple Choice English Comprehension and Standard English Comprehension papers.

This book has been written with the aim of helping students practise their comprehension skills as a way of improving their abilities to understand written information.

The tests contained in this book have been prepared for children in school years 4, 5 and 6, ages 8 – 11 years old. As well as being helpful for general revision and practice, these comprehension tests are written to particularly assist students who are preparing for entrance examinations at 11+ for grammar schools and independent schools.

How to use this book

This book contains important, practical advice on the best ways to approach standard comprehension tests and how to write effective and purposeful answers. The book also provides tips and advice for writing compositions/essays. These are writing tests that cover aspects of creative writing such as stories, reports and letters.

Five standard comprehension tests are provided, each with a reading passage followed by questions that are answered by the students on the papers provided.

Each of the five comprehension tests is accompanied by a composition/essay test that provides a choice of two tasks for the student to attempt.

A clear, helpful and detailed marking scheme is provided for both the comprehension test and compositions to enable an accurate assessment to be made of each student's performance.

www.tutormaster-services.co.uk www.tutormaster-services.co.uk www.tutormaster-services.co.uk www.tutormaster-services.co.uk

www.tutormaster-services.co.uk www.tutormaster-services.co.uk www.tutormaster-services.co.uk www.tutormaster-services.co.uk

Tutor Master Services

ENGLISH
Comprehension

Standard

Tips and Advice
for completing
Comprehensions and Compositions

www.tutormaster-services.co.uk
© 2015 Tutor Master Services

www.tutormaster-services.co.uk

www.tutormaster-services.co.uk

Comprehension Tips

It is a good idea for the student to read through this advice with an adult before they begin the comprehension papers.

- Read the story passage carefully as it is important you understand it. Remember as much as you can. (It may help if you think of your brain as a sponge, soaking up as many details as you can!)
- Read the question carefully then do **exactly** as it says, e.g., if the question asks you to answer in your **own words**, make sure you do.
- Always answer in **full sentences** unless you are told not to.
- It is important that you understand that you are allowed to go back and check the reading passage to help you answer the questions. In fact it is **essential** to use the reading passage to help. This exam is not a memory test.
- When you answer, use words and phrases from the passage as **evidence** to back up your ideas.
- If you use words from the passage as evidence to help explain your answer, make sure you put the words you use in quotation marks (" ").
- If a question asks you to explain a word and you are not sure what it means, go back to the passage and read the sentences that come before and after the word you need to explain. Use the **context** in which the word is used to have your best guess.
- Look at the marks being given for each question. Make sure you give enough **evidence** and **details** to get the number of marks being given.
- If the question has two parts make sure you give a two part answer to cover each part of the question.
- Present your work as neatly as you can and make sure you spell correctly, especially when words you are using are copied from the passage or question.
- Always try to write an answer for every question. If you do not answer you will lose marks. Always have a guess if you are unsure as you never know, you may be correct!
- Some questions are about grammar, spellings and parts of speech. To find out more about words and their meanings my book, *Tutor Master helps you Learn English - A Literacy Dictionary*, contains lots of helpful definitions and examples.

Practical Advice

- Agree a suitable time and place where the practice test will be carried out. It is advisable for the student to conduct the test in a place where they can be supervised and timed by an adult and which will also be free from noise or distractions.
- Provide a clock that the student can see, several pencils, a ruler and an eraser. It is probably better to write answers in pencil so that any mistakes can be more easily corrected.
- As this is a practice situation it is probably helpful to read through the instructions on the front page with the student before they begin.
- Make sure the student understands what they have to do before they begin and give them the chance to ask any questions.

Tips for Writing Compositions

These are general guidelines only. For more detailed advice and practical help with story writing, see *Tutor Master helps you Write Stories Book 1* and *Tutor Master helps you Write Stories Book 2*.

- When choosing a story to write in an exam it is a good idea to choose the title that you may be able to write from your own experience. This makes it easier as you know how the story begins, what happens and how it ends.

- It is **very important** to make sure that the story you write is about the title you have chosen or been given.

- Examiners often prefer you to show your writing skills by making your story sound true, even if it is made up. Amazing, improbable adventure stories are often difficult to complete in the half hour of writing time available.

- Try to think how your story will end **before** you start to write. It is very important that you finish the story. If you already know how it will end you can quickly bring it to a conclusion if you find you are running out of time.

- It is a good idea to write your stories in the **past tense** as you will find it easier to maintain this throughout the story.

- Make sure your story has a clear **beginning** where you set the scene and introduce the main ideas – this should be fairly short, maybe just one paragraph. Make sure the **middle** part of your story is the longest part containing two, three or more paragraphs. **End** your story with a fairly short concluding paragraph.

- Begin a new paragraph each time you change the topic you are writing about.

- Be careful to punctuate your work using the rules for punctuating written work.

- Be careful to spell correctly, especially those words you know you find difficult.

- Try to include some **direct speech** correctly punctuated using the rules for punctuating direct speech.

- Write good descriptions using adjectives, adverbs and similes.

- Try to describe your **feelings** or the **feelings** of the characters you are writing about.

www.tutormaster-services.co.uk
© 2015 Tutor Master Services

Tutor Master Services

ENGLISH
Comprehension

Standard Introductory
Paper 1A

40 minutes

Read the following carefully:

1. This paper is in two parts – a comprehension and a composition (story). You should spend about half an hour on each part.

2. Start this test when you are told to do so.

3. You should read the passage and then answer the questions about it. It is a good idea to look back at the passage to check your answers as many times as you want.

4. You should aim to finish all the questions.

5. Work as quickly and as carefully as you can.

6. You will have 10 minutes reading time, 30 minutes to do the comprehension and 30 minutes for the composition.

Text © David Malindine

The right of David Malindine to be identified as author of this work has been asserted by him in accordance with the Copyright, Designs and Patents Act 1988.

Copyright © Tutor Master Services, 2015

All rights reserved, including translation. No part of this publication may be reproduced or transmitted in any form or by any means, electronic or mechanical, including photocopying, recording or duplication in any information storage and retrieval system, without permission in writing from the publishers, and may not be photocopied or otherwise reproduced without permission in writing from the publisher.

Published by:

Tutor Master Services, 61 Ashness Gardens, Greenford, Middlesex UB6 0RW.

ISBN: 978-0-9555909-7-9

Read the passage below and answer the following questions carefully. It is a good idea to go back and check the passage to find your answers. Write your answers neatly on the answer sheet.

Alice in Wonderland

Alice has been exploring down a rabbit hole following after a White Rabbit, when suddenly she finds herself falling. She falls slowly and for a long time until her fall is broken and with a thump! thump! she lands upon a heap of sticks and dry leaves and the fall is over.

5   Alice was not hurt at all and quickly jumped to her feet. She looked around but could see little as it was dark, but she could see the White Rabbit hurrying away down a long passage. Not wanting to see the White Rabbit disappear, Alice ran like the wind and as the White Rabbit turned a corner, Alice was just in time to hear it say, "Oh my ears and whiskers, how late it's
10 getting!" Although Alice was following close behind, when she turned the corner she could no longer see the Rabbit, and she found herself in a long, low hall, which was dimly lit up by a row of lamps hanging from the roof.

All around the hall were doors, and one by one Alice tried to open them but they were all locked. She walked sadly to the middle of the hall and stood
15 there wondering how she would ever get out.

Suddenly she came upon a little three-legged table made of solid glass, and on the top was placed a tiny golden key. Alice thought that this key must surely open one of the doors in the hall, but to her dismay she found that either the locks were too large or the key was too small, so she was unable
20 to unlock any of the doors. However, as she looked more carefully she noticed a low curtain that she had not seen before, and behind was a little door fifteen inches in height. She put the little golden key into the lock and to her great delight it fitted.

Alice opened the door and found that it led into a small passage. She knelt
25 down and looking along the passage she saw the most beautiful garden imaginable. Alice really wanted to get out of the gloomy hall and to wander about among the beds of bright flowers and cool fountains, but she could not even get her head through the doorway, "And even if my head *would* go through," thought poor Alice, "it would be of little use without my
30 shoulders. Oh, how I wish I could shut up like a telescope! I think I could if I only knew how to begin."

There seemed to be no use in waiting by the little door, so she went back to the table, half hoping she might find another key on it, or at any rate a book of rules for closing people up like telescopes. This time she found a little
35 bottle on the table, which Alice remembered had certainly not been there before. Tied around the neck of the bottle was a paper label with the words "DRINK ME" beautifully printed on it in large letters.

It was all very well to say, "Drink me," but the wise little Alice was not going to do *that* in a hurry. "No, I'll look first and see whether it's marked

www.tutormaster-services.co.uk   www.tutormaster-services.co.uk   www.tutormaster-services.co.uk   www.tutormaster-services.co.uk

40 'poison' or not"; for she had read several nice little stories about children who had got burnt and eaten up by wild beasts, and other unpleasant things all because they would not remember the simple rules their friends had taught them: such as, that a red-hot poker will burn you if you hold it too long; and that, if you cut your finger very deeply with a knife, it usually bleeds;

45 and she had never forgotten that, if you drink much from a bottle marked "poison" it is almost certain to make you ill sooner or later.

However this bottle was not marked "poison", so Alice tasted it and found it to be very nice, having mixed flavours of cherry-tart, custard, pineapple, roast turkey, toffee and hot buttered toast, and she very soon finished it off.

50 "What a curious feeling!" said Alice. "I must be shutting up like a telescope!"

And she was indeed: she was now only ten inches high, and her face brightened up at the thought that she was now the right size for going through the little door into that lovely garden.

First, however, she waited for a few minutes to see if she was going to

55 shrink any further: she felt a little nervous about this; "for it might end, you know, " said Alice to herself, "in my going out altogether like a candle. I wonder what I should be like then?"

From *Alice in Wonderland* by Charles Lutwidge Dodgson

© 2015 Tutor Master Services

ANSWER SECTION

PLEASE WRITE YOUR FULL NAME HERE:

_____

www.tutormaster-services.co.uk   www.tutormaster-services.co.uk   www.tutormaster-services.co.uk   www.tutormaster-services.co.uk   www.tutormaster-services.co.uk   www.tutormaster-services.co.uk   www.tutormaster-services.co.uk

MARKS

1. Alice was uninjured after her fall. Copy down the sentence from paragraph 2 (lines 5 - 12) that tells us this.   **3**

   ……………………………………………………………………………………

   ……………………………………………………………………………………

2. Two characters are mentioned in paragraph 1. Who are they?   **2**

   Character one …………………………………………………………………..

   Character two …………………………………………………………………..

3. Explain why Alice could see better in the low hall than in the long passage.   **3**

   ……………………………………………………………………………………

   ……………………………………………………………………………………

   ……………………………………………………………………………………

4. a) "Alice ran like the wind" (line 8).   What name do we give to this type of comparison?   **2**

   ……………………………………………………………………………………

   b) Rewrite the sentence using an adverb instead of the comparison.   **2**

   ……………………………………………………………………………………

   ……………………………………………………………………………………

5. Put a ring around the word which is closest in meaning to the word "dismay" (line 18) as it is used in the passage.   **2**

   pleasure   success   shock   joy

www.tutormaster-services.co.uk
© 2015 Tutor Master Services

6. The following is a list of events which happen in paragraph 4 (lines 16 - 23). They have been mixed up. You must try to put them back in order by writing numbers against each one. The first has been done for you.   **5**

Alice found a little three-legged table.   ....1....

She noticed a low curtain.   ....

She found a tiny golden key.   ....

She found the locks too big or the key too small. ....

She put the little golden key into the lock.   ....

She found a little door fifteen inches in height. ....

7. "Alice really wanted to get out of the gloomy hall and to wander about among the beds of bright flowers and cool fountains" (lines 26 - 27). From this phrase pick out three adjectives and the nouns that they describe.   **6**

Adjective	Noun

8. In your own words explain why Alice was unable to enter the beautiful garden.   **3**

....

....

....

9. a) What does Alice wish to become?   **3**

....

....

www.tutormaster-services.co.uk www.tutormaster-services.co.uk www.tutormaster-services.co.uk www.tutormaster-services.co.uk

www.tutormaster-services.co.uk www.tutormaster-services.co.uk www.tutormaster-services.co.uk www.tutormaster-services.co.uk

b) Explain why she may wish for this.

3

....

....

....

....

....

10. What were the instructions printed on the bottle label?

3

....

11. Why did Alice hesitate before following the instructions?

3

....

....

....

....

....

....

12. Explain fully why Alice was relieved when she tasted the contents of the bottle.

3

....

....

....

....

....

13. Put a ring around the word which is closest in meaning to the word "curious" (line 50) as it is used in the passage.

3

angry   peculiar   serious   frightening

© 2015 Tutor Master Services

www.tutormaster-services.co.uk

14. "What a curious feeling!" said Alice. "I must be shutting up like a telescope!" (line 50).

4

Alice was both happy and nervous about this experience. Read the last two paragraphs and then in your own words explain why she felt like this.

....

....

....

....

....

....

....

....

....

TOTAL MARKS =   50

END OF QUESTIONS ON PART ONE

© 2015 Tutor Master Services

Tutor Master Services

ENGLISH
Composition/Essay

30 minutes
Total Marks: 50

Choose one of these to write

1. Imagine that Alice is now able to enter the beautiful garden that she can see at the end of the passage. In the garden she meets the White Rabbit.

   Write the speech conversation that takes place between them remembering that Alice will be keen to find out all she can about where she is and who is the mysterious rabbit. Use the title "**Speech Conversation between Alice and the White Rabbit**"

   You should aim to write 15 - 20 lines. Do <u>NOT</u> write a play script but set out your work neatly following the punctuation rules for direct speech.

   OR

2. Write a story based on this title.

   "**The Garden**"

   You could write about some gardens you have visited or your own garden. If you write about your own garden, consider describing the size, shape and layout; what you do in the garden; what your parents do in the garden; what you do together in the garden; what you do if your friends come to play and what you would miss if you didn't have a garden.

- Remember that the examiners are looking to see if you have included speech correctly punctuated, feelings (of yourself or your characters) and good description.

- Remember to check your grammar, spelling and punctuation carefully.

- Write on lined paper.

www.tutormaster-services.co.uk   www.tutormaster-services.co.uk   www.tutormaster-services.co.uk

....
....
....
....
....
....
....
....
....
....
....
....
....
....
....
....
....
....
....
....
....
....
....
....

www.tutormaster-services.co.uk
© 2015 Tutor Master Services

www.tutormaster-services.co.uk www.tutormaster-services.co.uk www.tutormaster-services.co.uk
www.tutormaster-services.co.uk www.tutormaster-services.co.uk www.tutormaster-services.co.uk www.tutormaster-services.co.uk

....

....

....

....

....

....

....

....

....

....

....

....

....

....

....

....

....

....

....

....

....

....

....

www.tutormaster-services.co.uk
© 2015 Tutor Master Services

www.tutormaster-services.co.uk
© 2015 Tutor Master Services

www.tutormaster-services.co.uk   www.tutormaster-services.co.uk   www.tutormaster-services.co.uk   www.tutormaster-services.co.uk   www.tutormaster-services.co.uk

www.tutormaster-services.co.uk   www.tutormaster-services.co.uk   www.tutormaster-services.co.uk   www.tutormaster-services.co.uk   www.tutormaster-services.co.uk

*Tutor**M**aster**S**ervices*

ENGLISH
Comprehension

Standard Introductory
Paper 1B

40 minutes

Read the following carefully:

1. This paper is in two parts – a comprehension and a composition (story). You should spend about half an hour on each part.

2. Start this test when you are told to do so.

3. You should read the passage and then answer the questions about it. It is a good idea to look back at the passage to check your answers as many times as you want.

4. You should aim to finish all the questions.

5. Work as quickly and as carefully as you can.

6. You will have 10 minutes reading time, 30 minutes to do the comprehension and 30 minutes for the composition.

Text © David Malindine

The right of David Malindine to be identified as author of this work has been asserted by him in accordance with the Copyright, Designs and Patents Act 1988.

Copyright © Tutor Master Services, 2015

All rights reserved, including translation. No part of this publication may be reproduced or transmitted in any form or by any means, electronic or mechanical, including photocopying, recording or duplication in any information storage and retrieval system, without permission in writing from the publishers, and may not be photocopied or otherwise reproduced without permission in writing from the publisher.

Published by:

Tutor Master Services, 61 Ashness Gardens, Greenford, Middlesex UB6 0RW.

ISBN: 978-0-9555909-7-9

Read the passage below and answer the following questions carefully. It is a good idea to go back and check the passage to find your answers. Write your answers neatly on the answer sheet.

Peter Pan

The Story of Peter Pan is about a boy who was lost by his parents when he was young and who never grows up. He comes from the Never Land, an island which children sometimes visit in their dreams. The most magical thing about Peter Pan is ... he can fly. In the part of the story which comes next, Peter Pan has arrived at
5 *a large house in London.*

Sometimes when Peter Pan was lonely, he would fly down to a large house in London which was the home of Mr and Mrs Darling, parents of Wendy, Michael and John. Peter Pan liked to visit their home and he would fly up to the nursery window and peep inside. Sometimes, Mrs Darling would be
10 reading a story to her children and Peter would listen at the window. He would remember with gladness, and a little sadness, what it was like to be part of a human family and to have a mother.

One night the nursery windows had been left open so Peter flew straight into the room where the children were sleeping. To his dismay the family
15 pet dog Nana (who strangely was also the children's nurse) came bounding into the nursery and Peter had to make a rapid exit. As he tried to escape, his shadow got caught on the window catch and he had to leave it behind. Later, Mrs Darling found the shadow on the floor and locked it in a drawer.

The very next evening when Mr and Mrs Darling were out, Peter sent
20 Tinker Bell, his tiny fairy friend, to search for his shadow. She looked in all the cupboards, she hunted under the beds, she even delved inside a jug. Eventually she found the shadow in the drawer where it had been placed, just as Peter flew in through the window. He grabbed his shadow and searched around trying to find something which would stick his shadow
25 back on.

All the noise woke Wendy up. She was rather surprised to find Peter Pan in the nursery, but she recognised him as a boy she had seen in her dreams. She took her workbox and carefully and neatly stitched the shadow on again.

30 John and Michael then woke up and joined Wendy. They listened spellbound as Peter told them about his fierce fight with the Pirates on Never Land and the Mermaids with long tails which swam in the seas near the island. Peter painted a picture of excitement and adventure which the children found hard to resist. And of course they wanted to go.

35 So it was agreed that they should first learn to fly and then go away with Peter Pan that very night.

"Can you teach us to fly, Peter?" the children begged.

"Of course, it's easy," Peter replied as he flew around the room.

© 2015 Tutor Master Services

www.tutormaster-services.co.uk   www.tutormaster-services.co.uk   www.tutormaster-services.co.uk   www.tutormaster-services.co.uk

www.tutormaster-services.co.uk   www.tutormaster-services.co.uk   www.tutormaster-services.co.uk   www.tutormaster-services.co.uk

40 It looked delightfully easy so the children tried jumping from the bed but they went down instead of up!

"Oh, please show us how!" the children cried.

"You just think lovely wonderful thoughts," Peter explained, "and they lift you up in the air."

45 However, Peter had been teasing them, for no-one can fly unless the fairy dust has been blown on them. Peter had some on his hands and he blew some on them with the most superb results.

Michael let go of the bed he had been holding on to and immediately floated across the room.

"I flewed!" he shouted happily whilst still in mid-air.

50 After a great deal of practice they were ready to leave. Not a moment too soon, for running up the stairs came Mr and Mrs Darling.

One by one the children flew out of the nursery window, leaving their poor parents behind. Soon they were soaring through the night sky with the lights of London far below them.

From *Peter Pan* by J M Barrie

© 2015 Tutor Master Services

www.tutormaster-services.co.uk www.tutormaster-services.co.uk www.tutormaster-services.co.uk
www.tutormaster-services.co.uk www.tutormaster-services.co.uk www.tutormaster-services.co.uk www.tutormaster-services.co.uk

ANSWER SECTION

PLEASE WRITE YOUR FULL NAME HERE:

_____

MARKS

1. Who is the main character mentioned in the second paragraph (lines 6 - 12)?

    2

    ....

2. Name the five other characters mentioned in paragraph 2

    5

    ....

    ....

    ....

3. In paragraph 2 (lines 6 - 12) five different verbs are used to describe what Peter Pan liked to do. List the verbs here.

    5

    1) ....   4) ....

    2) ....   5) ....

    3) ....

4. In your own words explain why Peter Pan "would remember with gladness, and a little sadness, what it was like to be part of a human family and to have a mother".

    3

    ....

    ....

    ....

    ....

    ....

    ....

    ....

© 2015 Tutor Master Services

www.tutormaster-services.co.uk   www.tutormaster-services.co.uk

www.tutormaster-services.co.uk   www.tutormaster-services.co.uk   www.tutormaster-services.co.uk

5. What was unusual about the family pet dog Nana?   **3**

   ....

   ....

   ....

6. Put a ring around the word which is closest in meaning to the word "rapid"   **2**
   (line 16) as it is used in the passage.

        slow   gentle   sad   hasty

7. The following is a list of events which happen in the 3rd paragraph (lines 13 - 18).   **5**
   They have been mixed up. You must try to put them back in order by writing the
   numbers 2 - 6 against each one. The first has been done for you.

   Mrs Darling locked the shadow in a drawer.   ....

   Nana came bounding into the nursery.   ....

   Peter's shadow got caught on a window catch.   ....

   Peter made a rapid exit.   ....

   The nursery windows were left open.   .....**1**....

   Peter flew into the room.   ....

8. From paragraph 4 (lines 19 - 25) pick out three verbs that are used to tell how   **3**
   Tinker Bell searches for Peter Pan's shadow.

   1) ....

   2) ....

   3) ....

9. Put a ring around the word which is closest in meaning to the word "grabbed"   **2**
   (line 23) as it is used in the passage.

        threw   shoved   snatched   placed

www.tutormaster-services.co.uk www.tutormaster-services.co.uk www.tutormaster-services.co.uk

www.tutormaster-services.co.uk www.tutormaster-services.co.uk www.tutormaster-services.co.uk www.tutormaster-services.co.uk

10. Although Wendy was "rather surprised" (line 26) to find Peter Pan in the nursery, she was not scared. Copy down the phrase which explains her reaction.   **3**

....

....

11. a) Where was Peter Pan's home?   **3**

....

b) Copy out the sentence found in the 6th paragraph (lines 30 - 34) which tells how Peter Pan persuaded the children to accompany him home.   **3**

....

....

....

12. At first, despite their efforts, the children could not fly. What did Peter do that eventually helped them succeed?   **3**

....

....

....

13. In line 49, Michael in his excitement, wrongly expresses the past tense of the verb. Write down what he should have said if he had spoken correctly.   **3**

....

....

....

© 2015 Tutor Master Services

14. In your own words explain the different feelings experienced by the children and Mr and Mrs Darling at the end of the passage.

5

....

....

....

....

....

....

....

....

TOTAL MARKS =   **50**

END OF QUESTIONS ON PART ONE

© 2015 Tutor Master Services

T u t o r M a s t e r S e r v i c e s

ENGLISH
Composition/Essay

30 minutes
Total Marks: 50

Choose one of these to write

1. Imagine you are a newspaper reporter and you have been asked to write a report to tell the story of the missing children. You visit the home of Mr and Mrs Darling to collect information and details about what happened.

    Use these ideas to write paragraphs to report this news story "**Missing Children in Fly Away Mystery**":

    a) The background to the event including who was involved and any suspicions that Mr and Mrs Darling had that something may have been wrong.

    b) An exciting description of what happened when the children left the house.

    c) An account from Mr and Mrs Darling where they explain their feelings about their children's disappearance.

    Remember to write clearly and in an interesting way so that the reader will have a real sense of excitement as you describe what happened.

    OR

2. Write a story based on a journey you have made. This may involve flying in an aeroplane or helicopter if you wish but it does not have to. Use the title

    "**The Amazing Journey**"

*   Remember that the examiners are looking to see if you have included speech correctly punctuated, feelings (of yourself or your characters) and good description.

*   Remember to check your grammar, spelling and punctuation carefully.

www.tutormaster-services.co.uk   www.tutormaster-services.co.uk

www.tutormaster-services.co.uk   www.tutormaster-services.co.uk   www.tutormaster-services.co.uk

www.tutormaster-services.co.uk
© 2015 Tutor Master Services

www.tutormaster-services.co.uk
© 2015 Tutor Master Services

....
....
....
....
....
....
....
....
....
....
....
....
....
....
....
....
....
....
....
....
....
....
....

www.tutormaster-services.co.uk

TutorMasterServices

ENGLISH
Comprehension

Standard Introductory
Paper 1C

40 minutes

Read the following carefully:

1. This paper is in two parts – a comprehension and a composition (story). You should spend about half an hour on each part.

2. Start this test when you are told to do so.

3. You should read the passage and then answer the questions about it. It is a good idea to look back at the passage to check your answers as many times as you want.

4. You should aim to finish all the questions.

5. Work as quickly and as carefully as you can.

6. You will have 10 minutes reading time, 30 minutes to do the comprehension and 30 minutes for the composition.

Text © David Malindine

The right of David Malindine to be identified as author of this work has been asserted by him in accordance with the Copyright, Designs and Patents Act 1988.

Copyright © Tutor Master Services, 2015

All rights reserved, including translation. No part of this publication may be reproduced or transmitted in any form or by any means, electronic or mechanical, including photocopying, recording or duplication in any information storage and retrieval system, without permission in writing from the publishers, and may not be photocopied or otherwise reproduced without permission in writing from the publisher.

Published by:

Tutor Master Services, 61 Ashness Gardens, Greenford, Middlesex UB6 0RW.

ISBN: 978-0-9555909-7-9

www.tutormaster-services.co.uk

Read the passage below and answer the following questions carefully. It is a good idea to go back and check the passage to find your answers. Write your answers neatly on the answer sheet.

The Wizard of Oz

Dorothy lived with Uncle Henry and Aunt Em on a farm in Kansas, America. Life was hard for them but they were kind and hardworking. Dorothy had a pet, a little black dog called Toto, with whom she played and had fun. One day a cyclone – a strong and powerful wind – blew fiercely across the land and carried their house

5 *away with Dorothy and Toto sheltering inside.*

The house whirled around two or three times and rose slowly through the air. Dorothy felt as if she were going up in a balloon.

Dorothy did not know that their house was at the exact spot where the north and south winds met, which made it the exact centre of the cyclone. She

10 just managed to grab Toto before the whole house started shaking. Next minute, it rose up in the air, higher and higher until it was at the very top of the cyclone; and there it remained and was carried along as if it were a wind blown feather.

It was very dark, and the wind howled horribly around her, but Dorothy

15 soon got used to riding along. She felt as if she were being rocked in a cradle. At last she crawled over the swaying floor to her bed and lay down upon it; Toto followed and lay down beside her.

In spite of the swaying of the house and the wailing of the wind, Dorothy soon closed her eyes and fell asleep.

20 Dorothy was awakened by the bright sunshine coming in through the window and flooding the little room with light. The house was no longer moving, for the cyclone had set the house down very gently, in the midst of a country of marvellous beauty. She sprang from her bed, and with Toto at her heels, ran and opened the door.

25 The little girl gave a cry of amazement and looked about her, her eyes growing bigger and bigger at the wonderful sights she saw. She could see a beautiful place with fruit trees, beds of gorgeous flowers and colourful birds whose brilliant plumage flashed and glittered. A little way off was a small brook, whose waters rushed and sparkled along between green banks.

30 While Dorothy stood gazing at the beautiful sights she noticed, coming towards her, four strange little folk. They seemed about as tall as Dorothy, although they were, from their appearance, many years older.

Three were men, one a woman and all were oddly dressed. The three little men wore blue tall pointed hats with bells around the brims that tinkled

35 sweetly as they moved. They were dressed in blue, of the same shade as their hats and wore well-polished boots. The little woman's hat was white, and she wore a white gown that hung from her shoulders; over it were sprinkled little stars that glistened in the sun like diamonds.

40 The woman walked up to Dorothy, made a low bow and said, "Welcome to the land of the Munchkins. I am the Good Witch of the North. We are so grateful to you for having killed the Wicked Witch of the East and for setting our people free from bondage."

Dorothy listened to this speech with wonder and surprise. What could the little woman mean by saying she had killed the Wicked Witch of the
45 East? Dorothy was an innocent, harmless little girl, who had never killed anything in her life.

Dorothy was uncertain how to reply but she said, "You are very kind; but there must be some mistake. I have not killed anything."

"Your house did, anyway, " replied the little woman with a laugh, "and that
50 is the same thing. See!" she continued, pointing to the corner of the house, "there are her two toes, still sticking out from under a block of wood."

Dorothy looked, and gave a little cry of fright. There, just under the corner of the great beam the house rested on, two feet were sticking out, shod in silver shoes with pointed toes. "Oh dear! Oh dear!" cried Dorothy, clasping
55 her hands together in dismay, "the house must have fallen on her. Whatever shall we do?"

"There is nothing to be done," said the little woman calmly.

"But who was she?" asked Dorothy.

"She was the Wicked Witch of the East," answered the little woman. "She
60 has held all the Munchkins in bondage for many years, making them slave for her night and day. Now we are all set free and we are grateful to you for the favour."

From *The Wonderful Wizard of Oz* by L. Frank Baum

www.tutormaster-services.co.uk www.tutormaster-services.co.uk www.tutormaster-services.co.uk

www.tutormaster-services.co.uk www.tutormaster-services.co.uk www.tutormaster-services.co.uk

ANSWER SECTION

PLEASE WRITE YOUR FULL NAME HERE:

....

MARKS

1. Who is the principal character in this story?

    ....

1

2. In the second paragraph (lines 6 - 7), the movement of the house is described using two verbs accompanied by two adverbs. Copy them down.

    Verb 1 .... Adverb 1 ....

    Verb 2 .... Adverb 2 ....

4

3. What is a cyclone?

    ....

    ....

2

4. In paragraphs 2 and 3 (lines 6 - 13) the writer uses two similes. Copy them down.

    1) ....

       ....

    2) ....

       ....

4

5. The next two paragraphs (lines 14 - 19) describe how the house flies through the air. Pick out and write down four things that make this experience particularly unpleasant for Dorothy.

    1) ....

    2) ....

    3) ....

    4) ....

4

www.tutormaster-services.co.uk
© 2015 Tutor Master Services

6. Find and copy down exactly the sentence that explains how Dorothy was woken up.   **2**

   ....

   ....

   ....

   ....

7. Three verbs are used to tell Dorothy's first reactions to waking up. Write them down.   **3**

   1) ....

   2) ....

   3) ....

8. In the 7th paragraph (lines 25 - 29) Dorothy is astonished to see the beauty of the natural world. Write down four particular things from nature that she sees.   **4**

   1) ....

   2) ....

   3) ....

   4) ....

9. Write down one similarity and one difference that Dorothy notices between herself and the four strange little folk, when they first meet.

   Similarity **2**

   ....

   ....

   Difference..   **2**

   ....

   ....

© 2015 Tutor Master Services

www.tutormaster-services.co.uk   www.tutormaster-services.co.uk   www.tutormaster-services.co.uk

www.tutormaster-services.co.uk   www.tutormaster-services.co.uk   www.tutormaster-services.co.uk

10. The woman and men are dressed differently (lines 33 - 38). Pick out from the list the different descriptions and match each one with the woman or the men.

    Choose from the box below.

blue tall pointed hats - white gown - little stars - bells around the brims - white hat - dressed in blue - glistened like diamonds - well-polished boots

    8

Men	Woman
1)	
2)	
3)	
4)	

11. Put a ring around the word which is closest in meaning to the word "bondage" (line 42) as it is used in the passage.

    2

    bandage   misery   evil   slavery

12. What is Dorothy surprised to have found she has done?

    3

    ....

    ....

    ....

© 2015 Tutor Master Services

www.tutormaster-services.co.uk   www.tutormaster-services.co.uk   www.tutormaster-services.co.uk   www.tutormaster-services.co.uk   www.tutormaster-services.co.uk   www.tutormaster-services.co.uk

13. The following is a list of events which happen in the paragraphs (lines 39 - 57). They have been mixed up. You must try to put them back in order by writing the numbers 2 - 6 against each one. The first one has been done for you.

5

The woman says that nothing can be done. ………

Dorothy was uncertain how to reply. ………

The woman welcomed Dorothy. …1…

Dorothy clasped her hands together. ………

Dorothy listened with wonder and surprise. ………

The woman pointed to a corner of the house. ………

14. Using words and phrases from the three paragraphs (lines 39 - 48) explain why Dorothy is surprised and frightened by what has happened, while the little woman is grateful.

4

....

....

....

....

....

....

TOTAL MARKS = **50**

END OF QUESTIONS ON PART ONE

© 2015 Tutor Master Services

Tutor Master Services

ENGLISH
Composition/Essay

30 minutes
Total Marks: 50

Choose one of these to write

1. In the comprehension passage you have read, Dorothy and her house are blown into the air and carried away by a strong wind called a cyclone.

    You may also have experienced a day when the weather was really amazing. Use the title "**Amazing Weather**" to write a story/composition about such a day. You should say whether it was very hot and sunny, very cold, icy and snowy or even windy and stormy. You will need to describe the effect the weather had on you and the people you were with.

    OR

2. Imagine that you are Dorothy at the end of the comprehension passage you have read. You feel you must write a letter to Uncle Henry and Aunt Em who are left behind in America, to explain what has happened to you.

    Use your imagination to write a letter explaining: how you were carried away, your journey, what you found when you arrived and the accident involving the Wicked Witch of the East. Use the title "**Dorothy's Letter to Uncle Henry and Aunt Em**".

*   Remember to check your grammar, spelling and punctuation carefully.
*   Write on lined paper.
*   If you make a mistake, cross it out neatly and write in your correction.

....

....

....

....

....

....

....

....

....

....

....

....

....

....

....

....

....

....

....

....

....

www.tutormaster-services.co.uk
© 2015 Tutor Master Services

....

....

....

....

....

....

....

....

....

....

....

....

....

....

....

....

....

....

....

....

....

....

....

....

www.tutormaster-services.co.uk
© 2015 Tutor Master Services

TutorMasterServices

ENGLISH
Comprehension

Standard Introductory
Paper 1D

40 minutes

Read the following carefully:

1. This paper is in two parts – a comprehension and a composition (story). You should spend about half an hour on each part.

2. Start this test when you are told to do so.

3. You should read the passage and then answer the questions about it. It is a good idea to look back at the passage to check your answers as many times as you want.

4. You should aim to finish all the questions.

5. Work as quickly and as carefully as you can.

6. You will have 10 minutes reading time, 30 minutes to do the comprehension and 30 minutes for the composition.

Text © David Malindine

The right of David Malindine to be identified as author of this work has been asserted by him in accordance with the Copyright, Designs and Patents Act 1988.

Copyright © Tutor Master Services, 2015

All rights reserved, including translation. No part of this publication may be reproduced or transmitted in any form or by any means, electronic or mechanical, including photocopying, recording or duplication in any information storage and retrieval system, without permission in writing from the publishers, and may not be photocopied or otherwise reproduced without permission in writing from the publisher.

Published by:

Tutor Master Services, 61 Ashness Gardens, Greenford, Middlesex UB6 0RW.

ISBN: 978-0-9555909-7-9

www.tutormaster-services.co.uk www.tutormaster-services.co.uk
www.tutormaster-services.co.uk www.tutormaster-services.co.uk www.tutormaster-services.co.uk www.tutormaster-services.co.uk

Read the passage below and answer the following questions carefully. It is a good idea to go back and check the passage to find your answers. Write your answers neatly on the answer sheet.

Gulliver's Travels

Lemuel Gulliver had studied hard to become a doctor in London in the 17th Century. However, his business was unsuccessful and he chose instead to become a doctor on board a sailing ship. In early May 1699, he set sail on a ship called the Antelope.

5   The voyage to the South Seas went well for the first few weeks. Then there was a great storm, the ship hit a rock and was wrecked. Fortunately, Gulliver was a strong swimmer and he swam for as long as he could, until at last, when he could swim no further his feet touched the bottom of the seabed. He waded through the water to the shore and then completely
10 exhausted, he dragged himself up the beach, before lying down on a grassy bank where he fell fast asleep.

When daylight came, Gulliver opened his eyes. He lay still for a moment, wondering where he was, then he tried to sit up and look around. To his amazement he found he could not move his arms, his legs or even his head.
15 He was tied to the ground.

Suddenly, he felt something alive walking up his right leg and across his chest – like a mouse or a beetle. As he looked down he saw a tiny man about six inches high holding a bow and arrow in his hand. Suddenly, many more of the tiny men ran all over him. Gulliver let out an astonished
20 roar of surprise that startled the little men so much that they ran away in fright.

As Gulliver moved his head to look, he broke some of the strings that tied his left arm to the ground. This made the little men even more frightened and they shot many of their sharp arrows at him. Some arrows fell on his
25 face and hands, pricking like needles and hurting him.

Gulliver decided to lie still so as not to frighten the little people again. After a while, when they saw that he was not going to hurt them, they cut some of the strings that bound Gulliver's head so that he could move more freely. He could now see that the little people had built a tall wooden tower beside
30 his head which their tiny Emperor had climbed up and began to speak to Gulliver. But the little folk spoke a different language and Gulliver could not understand him at all. However, the Emperor realised that by now Gulliver must be hungry and he gave orders for food to be brought.

Ladders were put up against Gulliver's sides and cartloads of food and
35 wine arrived, which were carried up for him to eat and drink. The hungry, thirsty Gulliver drank a whole barrel of their wine in one gulp, and the tiny loaves of bread he ate three at a time. The little people stared at Gulliver in disbelief, as they did not believe it was possible to eat and drink so much. The Lilliputians (for that is what the little folk were called) kept bringing
40 more and more food and wine until Gulliver was so full up, he fell asleep.

www.tutormaster-services.co.uk   www.tutormaster-services.co.uk   www.tutormaster-services.co.uk

www.tutormaster-services.co.uk   www.tutormaster-services.co.uk   www.tutormaster-services.co.uk

45 When he woke up, Gulliver found himself lying on a kind of platform with wheels and he was being moved slowly along. Whilst he had been asleep, five hundred carpenters had made the wheeled, wooden platform and nine hundred men had hoisted Gulliver onto it. Then with five hundred guards either side and one thousand five hundred horses pulling hard, they began to move him towards their capital city about half a mile away.

50 It took a whole day and night to reach their destination, but at last the procession came to a halt outside a large temple that was no longer used. Since this was the largest building in the whole country, the Emperor had decided this was where Gulliver was to live – although it seemed as small as a dog kennel to him. The door was just big enough for him to creep through, and once inside he could only lie down.

55 The tiny Emperor of Lilliput did not intend setting Gulliver free altogether. He ordered his blacksmiths to put nearly a hundred of their tiny chains around his left leg, so that while he was able to move around, he could not go very far.

From *Gulliver's Travels* by Jonathan Swift

www.tutormaster-services.co.uk
© 2015 Tutor Master Services

ANSWER SECTION

PLEASE WRITE OUT YOUR FULL NAME HERE:

_____

MARKS

1. a) Write down the full name of the main character in this story.

    1

    ....

    b) Write down the name of the sailing ship mentioned in the first paragraph (lines 1 - 4).

    1

    ....

2. Copy down the sentence from paragraph 2 that tells us that the voyage was hit by disaster.

    3

    ....

    ....

    ....

    ....

    ....

3. Put a ring around the word which is closest in meaning to the word "waded" (line 9) as it is used in the passage.

    3

    strolled   swam   paddled   surfed

4. In your own words explain why Gulliver was unable to move when he woke up.

    3

    ....

    ....

    ....

    ....

    ....

www.tutormaster-services.co.uk www.tutormaster-services.co.uk www.tutormaster-services.co.uk
www.tutormaster-services.co.uk www.tutormaster-services.co.uk www.tutormaster-services.co.uk www.tutormaster-services.co.uk

5. Copy out the phrase from the fourth paragraph (lines 16 - 21) that tells us that Gulliver was unprepared for what had happened to him.

3

....

....

....

....

....

6. Paragraphs 5 & 6 (lines 22 - 33) describe some of the actions of both Gulliver and the Little People. Pick out from the list the different actions and match them with Gulliver or the Little People.

8

Choose from the box below

moved his head - became more frightened - lay still - broke some strings - shot sharp arrows - cut some strings - moved more freely - built a wooden tower

Gulliver	Little People
1)	
2)	
3)	
4)	

7. Why was Gulliver unable to understand what the Emperor was saying to him?

3

....

....

....

....

© 2015 Tutor Master Services

8. What was the real name for the little people?

   2

   ....

9. The following is a list of events which happen in paragraph 7 (lines 34 - 40). They have been mixed up. You must try to put them back in order by writing the numbers 1 - 5 against each one. The last one has been done for you.

   5

   Cartloads of food and wine arrived.   ....

   Gulliver fell asleep.   ....**6**...

   He ate three loaves of bread at a time.   ....

   Ladders were put up against Gulliver's sides. ....

   The little people stared in disbelief.   ....

   Gulliver drank a whole barrel of wine.   ....

10. Read and complete the following passage by putting in the correct words in the spaces. Choose words from the box below.

    3

    > one thousand five hundred - platform - nine hundred - five hundred - wheels - five hundred

    Gulliver woke up to find himself lying on a _____ on _____.

    Whilst he had been asleep _____ carpenters had constructed this.

    _____ men had lifted Gulliver onto it. It was guarded by

    _____ men on each side and it needed _____

    _____ horses to pull it.

11. Put a ring around the word or phrase which is closest in meaning to the word "destination" (line 47) as it is used in the passage.

    3

    place of origin   journey   journey's end   home

© 2015 Tutor Master Services

12. a) Although large, the temple seems small to Gulliver. Copy down the phrase that tells us this.   **3**

....

....

....

b) Look at the answer to 12a, what name do we give to this type of comparison?   **3**

....

13. The new living arrangements made for Gulliver (lines 47 - 56) were both good and bad. Pick out and explain some of the good points and bad points about how he had to live now.

Good points **3**

....

....

....

....

Bad points **3**

....

....

....

....

....

TOTAL MARKS =   **50**

END OF QUESTIONS ON PART ONE

www.tutormaster-services.co.uk   www.tutormaster-services.co.uk   www.tutormaster-services.co.uk

www.tutormaster-services.co.uk   www.tutormaster-services.co.uk   www.tutormaster-services.co.uk

T u t o r *M a s t e r* *S e r v i c e s*

ENGLISH
Composition/Essay

30 minutes
Total Marks: 50

Choose one of these to write

1. In the comprehension passage you have read, Gulliver is shipwrecked in a terrifying storm. After wading through the waters he collapses, exhausted, on the sandy beach. His experience of the seaside is clearly not a good one.

   However, the seaside is not always like this. Write a story/composition using the title **"A Day at the Seaside"** where you describe a day you have spent at the seaside. This may have been in this country or when you have been abroad.

   • Remember that the examiners are looking to see if you have included speech correctly punctuated, feelings (of yourself or your characters) and good description.

   OR

2. Imagine that later in the story an interpreter is found who can translate the English/Lilliputian languages. Write a speech conversation that takes place between the Emperor of Lilliput and Gulliver remembering that the Emperor will want to know how and why Gulliver has arrived and Gulliver will be keen to know why he is being held captive and what may happen to him next. Use the title **"Speech Conversation between Gulliver and the Emperor"**.

   You should aim to write 15 - 20 lines. Do **NOT** write a play script but set out your work neatly following the punctuation rules for direct speech.

   • Remember to check your grammar, spelling and punctuation carefully.

   • Write on lined paper.

   • If you make a mistake, cross it out neatly and write in your correction.

www.tutormaster-services.co.uk   www.tutormaster-services.co.uk   www.tutormaster-services.co.uk

www.tutormaster-services.co.uk   www.tutormaster-services.co.uk   www.tutormaster-services.co.uk

....

....

....

....

....

....

....

....

....

....

....

....

....

....

....

....

....

....

....

....

....

....

....

www.tutormaster-services.co.uk   www.tutormaster-services.co.uk   www.tutormaster-services.co.uk   www.tutormaster-services.co.uk

www.tutormaster-services.co.uk   www.tutormaster-services.co.uk   www.tutormaster-services.co.uk   www.tutormaster-services.co.uk

www.tutormaster-services.co.uk
© 2015 Tutor Master Services

© 2015 Tutor Master Services

www.tutormaster-services.co.uk www.tutormaster-services.co.uk www.tutormaster-services.co.uk

www.tutormaster-services.co.uk www.tutormaster-services.co.uk www.tutormaster-services.co.uk

....

....

....

....

....

....

....

....

....

....

....

....

....

....

....

....

....

....

....

....

....

....

....

....

© 2015 Tutor Master Services

www.tutormaster-services.co.uk   www.tutormaster-services.co.uk   www.tutormaster-services.co.uk   www.tutormaster-services.co.uk
www.tutormaster-services.co.uk   www.tutormaster-services.co.uk   www.tutormaster-services.co.uk   www.tutormaster-services.co.uk

Tutor Master Services

ENGLISH
Comprehension

Standard Introductory
Paper 1E

40 minutes

Read the following carefully:

1. This paper is in two parts – a comprehension and a composition (story). You should spend about half an hour on each part.

2. Start this test when you are told to do so.

3. You should read the passage and then answer the questions about it. It is a good idea to look back at the passage to check your answers as many times as you want.

4. You should aim to finish all the questions.

5. Work as quickly and as carefully as you can.

6. You will have 10 minutes reading time, 30 minutes to do the comprehension and 30 minutes for the composition.

Text © David Malindine

The right of David Malindine to be identified as author of this work has been asserted by him in accordance with the Copyright, Designs and Patents Act 1988.

Copyright © Tutor Master Services, 2015

All rights reserved, including translation. No part of this publication may be reproduced or transmitted in any form or by any means, electronic or mechanical, including photocopying, recording or duplication in any information storage and retrieval system, without permission in writing from the publishers, and may not be photocopied or otherwise reproduced without permission in writing from the publisher.

Published by:

Tutor Master Services, 61 Ashness Gardens, Greenford, Middlesex UB6 0RW.

ISBN: 978-0-9555909-7-9

www.tutormaster-services.co.uk www.tutormaster-services.co.uk

www.tutormaster-services.co.uk www.tutormaster-services.co.uk www.tutormaster-services.co.uk

Read the passage below and answer the following questions carefully. It is a good idea to go back and check the passage to find your answers. Write your answers neatly on the answer sheet.

Dick Whittington and His Cat

Once upon a time there was a boy called Dick Whittington. His mother and father were dead and he had no-one to care for him. He lived in a village in the countryside and was very poor. One day he decided to leave the countryside and go to London to seek his fortune.

5 When people in the village spoke of London, they described it as a wonderful place, where all the people were rich, and even the streets were paved with gold. Dick thought that he would be able to pick up gold from the streets and then become very rich too.

The journey to London was long and tiring, and Dick often felt cold, hungry
10 and lonely. One day, feeling particularly exhausted, Dick stopped at a milestone for a rest. As he rested, a black cat suddenly appeared and when Dick left to continue his journey, the cat followed. Dick had made a friend.

When Dick arrived in London he couldn't believe his eyes. He was surprised to see so many people in the streets, and amazed to see all the fine buildings,
15 houses, shops and churches.

Feeling hungry and exhausted, Dick fell asleep, sheltered in the doorway of a large house, with the cat beside him.

Early the next morning Dick awoke to see a very grand looking man appearing from the house. Instead of scolding Dick, the man, who was very
20 rich, offered him work and lodgings. Dick's bed was in a cold, draughty attic at the top of the house. At night rats and mice would scurry across the floor, and they even ran over his bed. Dick was pleased he had his cat to chase the rats and mice away.

Now the rich man had many ships which sailed to distant lands, and one
25 day he told Dick to sell his cat to the captain of a ship, who needed a cat to chase away the rats on board. Dick was sad to see his cat go, but let her go he did.

Dick missed his cat and felt lonely without her. He wished he had never sent her away. The rats and mice had returned to his room, and now there
30 was no cat to chase them away. Dick became so unhappy that he made up his mind to run away. He packed up his few belongings and set off on his way. He had not gone far when the bells of Bow Church began to chime. It sounded to Dick as if the bells were singing this tune:

"Turn again, Whittington,
35   Lord Mayor of London,
        Turn again, Whittington,
        Thrice Mayor of London"

Dick thought that if he were to become Lord Mayor of London he should go back. So he returned to the rich man's house.

40   Meanwhile, Dick's cat was sailing the high seas, chasing the rats away, and being thoroughly spoilt by the ship's crew.

One day the ship docked in a far off land. Its King asked the captain of the ship, "Please let me buy this amazing creature from you as my palace is overrun with rats, and they are eating all my food."

45   "Do you mean the cat?" the captain asked in a surprised voice.

"Yes," replied the King. "We do not have cats in this country. I will give you half of my Kingdom for the cat." The captain agreed and sold the cat to the King.

The cat loved her new surroundings and had soon rid the palace of the rats.
50   The King was so pleased with the cat, that he gave the captain a fortune to give to Dick on his return to London.

With this fortune from the King, Dick married the rich man's beautiful daughter. Dick was now a wealthy man and soon became Lord Mayor of London. In fact, he was to become Lord Mayor of London three times, so
55   the rhyme played by the bells had been right after all.

© 2015 Tutor Master Services

www.tutormaster-services.co.uk www.tutormaster-services.co.uk www.tutormaster-services.co.uk www.tutormaster-services.co.uk

www.tutormaster-services.co.uk www.tutormaster-services.co.uk www.tutormaster-services.co.uk www.tutormaster-services.co.uk

© 2015 Tutor Master Services

www.tutormaster-services.co.uk   www.tutormaster-services.co.uk   www.tutormaster-services.co.uk   www.tutormaster-services.co.uk

www.tutormaster-services.co.uk   www.tutormaster-services.co.uk   www.tutormaster-services.co.uk   www.tutormaster-services.co.uk

ANSWER SECTION

PLEASE WRITE YOUR FULL NAME HERE:

_____

MARKS

1. This story may not be true. Copy out the phrase from the first paragraph (lines 1 - 4) which tells us this.   **2**

   Phrase …………………………………………………………………………..

2. From paragraph one (lines 1 - 4), give three reasons why Dick decided to leave his village and go to London.   **3**

   1) …………………………………………………………………………..

   2) …………………………………………………………………………..

   3) …………………………………………………………………………..

3. From paragraph two (lines 5 - 8), give three reasons why London seemed an attractive place to Dick.   **3**

   1) …………………………………………………………………………..

   2) …………………………………………………………………………..

   3) …………………………………………………………………………..

4. Put a ring around the word which is closest in meaning to the word "exhausted" (line 10) as it is used in the passage.   **3**

         happy   sad   cheerful   weary

5. Write down four feelings that Dick has in paragraph three (lines 9 - 12).   **4**

   1) …………………………………………………………………………..

   2) …………………………………………………………………………..

   3) …………………………………………………………………………..

   4) …………………………………………………………………………..

www.tutormaster-services.co.uk

6. Why did Dick feel happier when he continued his journey?   **3**

....

....

....

....

7. Pick out and write down the phrase from the fourth paragraph which tells us that Dick was astonished at what he saw in London.   **2**

....

....

....

    3

8. Put a ring around the word which is closest in meaning to the word "scurry" (line 21) as it is used in the passage.

     scamper   walk   trot   chase

    4

9. Explain why Dick was both pleased and a little disappointed by what the rich man offered him? (paragraph 6)

....

....

....

....

....

....

....

....

....

....

....

10. Why did Dick have to sell his cat?

3

....

....

....

....

11. Using words and phrases from paragraphs 7 and 8, explain fully how Dick felt after he had sold his cat.

4

....

....

....

....

....

....

12. Who is the important London person that Dick believes the bells predict he will become?

2

....

13. For each of the following statements copy out a phrase from the passage (lines 40 - 51) which means the same thing.

8

Statement	Phrase
Dick's cat was travelling the world's oceans.	
The cat was being pampered by the ship's crew.	
There were too many rats in the palace.	
The captain was given lots of money to give to Dick.	

www.tutormaster-services.co.uk

14. Write down three things that happened to Dick which show that he had become a successful man.

6

1) ....

....

2) ....

....

3) ....

....

TOTAL MARKS =   **50**

END OF QUESTIONS ON PART ONE

© 2015 Tutor Master Services

Tutor Master Services

ENGLISH
Composition/Essay

30 minutes
Total Marks: 50

Choose one of these to write

1. Imagine that you are Dick Whittington at the end of the comprehension passage you have read. Now rich and successful, you decide to write a letter to a childhood friend you remember from the village where you grew up.

    Use your imagination to write the letter Dick wrote. You will need to invent the friend's name then:
    a) Remind the person of your friendship and early life in the village.
    b) Explain why you had to leave and what happened to you in London.
    c) The series of events that led to your wealth and success.

    Use the title "**Dick's Letter to his friend**".

    OR

2. Imagine that one day you open a can of drink and out pops a genie who offers you a million pounds. Use the title "**If I Were a Rich Person**" to write a story/ composition about what you would do with the money and what may happen to you.

    You may wish to think about: what you would buy, whether you would spend it all and whether you would give any of it to other people. Perhaps you might give to charities, say which ones and how much. Consider too, any problems you may face.

*   Remember that the examiners are looking to see if you have included speech correctly punctuated, feelings (of yourself or your characters) and good description.

*   Remember to check your grammar, spelling and punctuation carefully.

*   If you make a mistake, cross it out neatly and write in your correction.

www.tutormaster-services.co.uk   www.tutormaster-services.co.uk

www.tutormaster-services.co.uk   www.tutormaster-services.co.uk   www.tutormaster-services.co.uk   www.tutormaster-services.co.uk

....

....

....

....

....

....

....

....

....

....

....

....

....

....

....

....

....

....

....

....

....

....

www.tutormaster-services.co.uk www.tutormaster-services.co.uk www.tutormaster-services.co.uk www.tutormaster-services.co.uk www.tutormaster-services.co.uk www.tutormaster-services.co.uk

....

....

....

....

....

....

....

....

....

....

....

....

....

....

....

....

....

....

....

....

....

....

www.tutormaster-services.co.uk
© 2015 Tutor Master Services

www.tutormaster-services.co.uk   www.tutormaster-services.co.uk   www.tutormaster-services.co.uk   www.tutormaster-services.co.uk

www.tutormaster-services.co.uk   www.tutormaster-services.co.uk   www.tutormaster-services.co.uk   www.tutormaster-services.co.uk

www.tutormaster-services.co.uk
© 2015 Tutor Master Services

Tutor M aster S ervices

ENGLISH
Comprehension

Answers and Marking Schemes
for
Standard Introductory
Papers 1 – 5
and
Compositions

© 2015 Tutor Master Services

Answers to Paper 1A

Question number	Answer	Mark	Parent's notes and additional comments
1	Alice was not hurt at all and quickly jumped to her feet. (line 1)	3	The whole sentence must be copied for 3 marks.
2	Alice The White Rabbit	1 1	
3	The low hall was lit up by a row of lamps hanging from the roof but the long passage was dark.	3	
4a	A simile (it uses the words "like" or "as")	2	
4b	Alice ran quickly, speedily, swiftly, briskly, rapidly, hurriedly, hastily.	2	Student should use any one from the list given or any other suitable adverb (adverbs often end in 'ly')
5	shock	2	
6	Alice found a little three-legged table. …1… She noticed a low curtain. …4… She found a tiny golden key. …2… She found the locks too big or the key too small. …3… She put the little golden key into the lock. …6… She found a little door fifteen inches in height. …5…	5	No mark given for **1** as this was given in the question.
7	Adjective / Noun: gloomy — hall; bright — flowers; cool — fountains	6	(1 mark for each correct answer.)
8	Alice was too big to fit through the small doorway, not even her head would fit through. Or The doorway was too small for Alice to fit through.	3	Use discretion – award a mark for any alternative sensible answer.
9a	Alice wishes she could become a telescope.	3	
9b	She would like to be able to become smaller as a telescope does when it closes up, shortens or compresses within itself. OR Alice wishes for this so that she becomes smaller and could fit through the door and then wander about in the beautiful garden.	3	Use discretion – award a mark for an answer that explains why Alice may want to be smaller.
10	DRINK ME	3	Does not need to be written in capital letters.

www.tutormaster-services.co.uk

English Comprehension Standard Introductory Set One Answers			
Question number	Answer	Mark	Parent's notes and additional comments
11	She hesitated as she remembered the simple rule which was always to check the bottle to see if it is marked "poison" before you drink from it. Then she checked to see if the bottle was marked "poison".	3	Use discretion and award marks for similar answers.
12	Alice was relieved when she tasted the contents of the bottle as it tasted very nice, with mixed flavours of cherry-tart, custard, pineapple, roast turkey, toffee and hot buttered toast.	3	Must explain fully to score full marks.
13	peculiar	3	
14	Alice was happy to be shutting up like a telescope as she had shrunk to only ten inches high and she knew she was now the right size to fit through the door and get into the garden. Alice was nervous about shutting up like a telescope because she thought she might shrink too far and she might disappear altogether. She wondered what she should be like then.	4	Use discretion to assess whether the student has understood why Alice has mixed feelings about what is happening to her. Encourage students to separate their answer into 2 parts.

Answers to Paper 1B

Question number	Answer	Mark	Parent's notes and additional comments
1	Peter Pan	2	
2	Mr Darling, Mrs Darling, Wendy, Michael and John	5	
3	fly, visit, peep, listen, remember	5	In any order
4	Peter Pan remembered with a little gladness how nice it was to be part of a human family with a mother and brothers and sisters. Peter Pan remembered with a little sadness, what it was like to be part of a human family because he did not have a mother now nor any other family members.	3	Use discretion to award marks for something similar. Encourage students to separate their answer into 2 parts.
5	Nana the dog was also the children's nurse.	3	
6	hasty	2	

www.tutormaster-services.co.uk
© 2015 Tutor Master Services

www.tutormaster-services.co.uk   www.tutormaster-services.co.uk   www.tutormaster-services.co.uk   www.tutormaster-services.co.uk

www.tutormaster-services.co.uk   www.tutormaster-services.co.uk   www.tutormaster-services.co.uk
www.tutormaster-services.co.uk   www.tutormaster-services.co.uk   www.tutormaster-services.co.uk   www.tutormaster-services.co.uk

English Comprehension Standard Introductory Set One Answers

Question number	Answer	Mark	Parent's notes and additional comments
7	Mrs Darling locked the shadow in a drawer. …6… Nana came bounding into the nursery. …3… Peter's shadow got caught on a window catch. …5… Peter made a rapid exit. …4… The nursery windows were left open. …1… Peter flew into the room. …2…	5	No mark given for **1** as this was given in the question.
8	looked, hunted, delved	3	In any order
9	snatched	2	
10	"She recognised him as a boy she had seen in her dreams."	3	
11a	Never Land	3	
11b	Peter Pan painted a picture of excitement and adventure which the children found hard to resist.	3	Use discretion to award marks for something similar.
12	Peter Pan helps the children to fly by blowing some fairy dust on them.	3	
13	"I flew"	3	
14	The feelings experienced by the children were excitement, pleasure, delight, joy, eagerness, amazement, astonishment (or similar) as they flew off to Never Land with the hope of great adventures. The feelings experienced by Mr and Mrs Darling were probably mixed e.g. surprise, astonishment, amazement and sad, sorrowful, miserable, heart broken at the sight of their children flying away from them. They probably wondered whether they would ever see them again.	5	Use discretion to award marks for something similar. Encourage students to separate their answer into 2 parts.

www.tutormaster-services.co.uk
 © 2015 Tutor Master Services

Answers to Paper 1C

Question number	Answer	Mark	Parent's notes and additional comments
1	Dorothy	1	
2	Verb 1) whirled Adverb 1) around Verb 2) rose Adverb 2) slowly	4	
3	A cyclone is a strong and powerful wind.	2	
4	Simile 1) as if she were going up in a balloon Simile 2) as if it were a wind blown feather	4	Answer can be in any order.
5	1) It was very dark. 2) The wind howled horribly. 3) The floor was swaying. 4) The house was swaying. 5) The wind was wailing.	4	1 mark each correct answer from those listed for a total of 4 marks. Answer can be in any order.
6	Dorothy was awakened by the bright sunshine coming in through the window and flooding the little room with light.	2	
7	Verb 1) sprang Verb 2) ran Verb 3) opened	3	
8	1) fruit <u>trees</u> 2) beds of <u>flowers</u> 3) colourful <u>birds</u> 4) a small <u>brook</u> (or <u>waters</u>)	4	Students must identify correctly the 4 nouns (underlined). Answer can be in any order.
9	Similarity - The people seemed as tall as Dorothy. Difference - The people appeared to be many years older.	2 2	1 similarity & 1 difference for 4 marks.

www.tutormaster-services.co.uk

Question number	Answer	Mark	Parent's notes and additional comments
10	<table><tr><th>Men</th><th>Woman</th></tr><tr><td>blue tall pointed hats</td><td>white gown</td></tr><tr><td>bells around the brims</td><td>little stars</td></tr><tr><td>dressed in blue</td><td>white hat</td></tr><tr><td>well-polished boots</td><td>glistened like diamonds</td></tr></table>	8	Answer can be in any order but must be in the correct columns.
11	slavery	2	
12	Dorothy is surprised to have found she has killed the Wicked Witch of the East	3	
13	The woman says that nothing can be done. …6… Dorothy was uncertain how to reply. …3… The woman welcomed Dorothy. …1… Dorothy clasped her hands together. …5… Dorothy listened with wonder and surprise. …2… The woman pointed to a corner of the house. …4…	5	
14	Dorothy is surprised because she did not know she had <u>killed the Wicked Witch of the East</u>. She is frightened because she was an <u>innocent, harmless little girl who had never killed anything in her life</u>. The woman is grateful to Dorothy for having <u>killed the Wicked Witch of the East and for setting the people free from bondage</u>.	4	For full marks the underlined phrases/words must be included.

© 2015 Tutor Master Services

Answers to Paper 1D

Question number	Answer	Mark	Parent's notes and additional comments
1a	Lemuel Gulliver	1	
1b	The Antelope	1	
2	Then there was a great storm, the ship hit a rock and was wrecked.	3	
3	paddled	3	
4	Gulliver was tied to the ground	3	
5	Gulliver let out an astonished roar of surprise.	3	
6	<table><tr><td>Gulliver</td><td>Little People</td></tr><tr><td>1) moved his head</td><td>became more frightened</td></tr><tr><td>2) lay still</td><td>shot sharp arrows</td></tr><tr><td>3) broke some strings</td><td>cut some strings</td></tr><tr><td>4) moved more freely</td><td>built a wooden tower</td></tr></table>	8	Answers can be in any order but must be in the correct column.
7	Gulliver was unable to understand the Emperor because he spoke a different language.	3	Use discretion to award marks for something similar.
8	Lilliputians	2	
9	Cartloads of food and wine arrived. ...2... Gulliver fell asleep. ...**6**... He ate three loaves of bread at a time. ...4... Ladders were put up against Gulliver's sides. ...1... The little people stared in disbelief. ...5... Gulliver drank a whole barrel of wine. ...3...	5	No mark given for **6** as this was given in the question.
10	Gulliver woke up to find himself lying on a **platform** on **wheels**. Whilst he had been asleep **five hundred** carpenters had constructed this. **Nine hundred** men had lifted Gulliver onto it. It was guarded by **five hundred** men on each side and it needed **one thousand five hundred** horses to pull it.	3	
11	journey's end	3	

www.tutormaster-services.co.uk www.tutormaster-services.co.uk www.tutormaster-services.co.uk

Question number	Answer	Mark	Parent's notes and additional comments
	English Comprehension Standard Introductory Set One Answers		
12a	it seemed as small as a dog kennel to him	3	
12b	a simile	3	
14	**Good points** The door was big enough for him to crawl through. He could lie down. He was able to move round. The temple was the largest building in the country.	3	Any 3 points for 3 marks.
	Bad points It was as small as a dog kennel. There was only enough room for him to lie down. He could not go very far. He had a hundred tiny chains around his left leg.	3	Any 3 points for 3 marks.

Answers to Paper 1E

Question number	Answer	Mark	Parent's notes and additional comments
1	Once upon a time	2	
2	1) His mother and father were dead. 2) He had no one to care for him. 3) He was very poor. 4) He wanted to seek his fortune in London	3	1 mark for each correct answer from those listed for a total of 3 marks.
3	1) It was a wonderful place. 2) All the people were rich. 3) Even the streets were paved with gold. 4) Dick could pick up gold from the street. 5) He could become very rich too.	3	1 mark for each correct answer from those listed for a total of 3 marks.
4	weary	3	
5	1) Dick felt cold. 2) Dick felt hungry. 3) Dick felt lonely. 4) Dick felt particularly exhausted.	4	
6	Dick felt happier when he continued his journey as the cat followed him and became his friend.	3	Use discretion to award marks for something similar.
7	He couldn't believe his eyes.	2	
8	scamper	3	

www.tutormaster-services.co.uk
© 2015 Tutor Master Services

www.tutormaster-services.co.uk   www.tutormaster-services.co.uk   www.tutormaster-services.co.uk

www.tutormaster-services.co.uk   www.tutormaster-services.co.uk   www.tutormaster-services.co.uk

English Comprehension Standard Introductory Set One Answers

Question number	Answer	Mark	Parent's notes and additional comments
9	Dick was pleased because the rich man offered him work and lodgings. Dick was disappointed because his bedroom was a cold, draughty attic and at night rats and mice would scurry across the floor and over his bed.	4	Use discretion to award marks for something similar. Encourage students to separate their answer into 2 parts.
10	Dick had to sell his cat because the rich man told him to. Also he had to sell it to the captain of a ship who needed a cat to chase away the rats on board.	3	
11	Dick missed his cat. He felt lonely without her. He wished he had never sent her away. Dick became very unhappy. He felt he wanted to run away.	4	Students <u>must</u> use words and phrases from the passage. Give one mark for each separate feeling mentioned.
12	The Lord Mayor of London	2	
13	<table><tr><th>Statement</th><th>Phrase</th></tr><tr><td>Dick's cat was travelling the world's ocean.</td><td>Dick's cat was sailing the high seas</td></tr><tr><td>The cat was being pampered by the ship's crew.</td><td>being thoroughly spoilt by the ship's crew</td></tr><tr><td>There were too many rats in the King's palace.</td><td>my palace is overrun with rats</td></tr><tr><td>The captain was given lots of money to give to Dick</td><td>he gave the captain a fortune to give to Dick</td></tr></table>	8	
14	1) Dick married the rich man's beautiful daughter. 2) Dick was now a wealthy man. 3) Dick soon became Lord Mayor of London	6	

www.tutormaster-services.co.uk
© 2015 Tutor Master Services

Marking scheme for Compositions

Technical Skills	Marks up to
How well does the story show evidence of a clear beginning, middle and end?	5
How well does the story give a sense of completion?	5
How well has punctuation been used (including paragraphing)?	5
How accurate is the spelling?	5
Overall impression of presentation (neatness, legibility, correction of errors, etc.).	2
Content and Quality	**Marks up to**
How well does the story reflect the requirements of the title given?	5
How well has the candidate used descriptive techniques, e.g., adjectives, adverbs, similes, to enhance the story?	6
How well has direct speech been used and punctuated correctly?	6
How well have the feelings of the character(s) been described?	5
How coherent is the story, i.e., does it flow from beginning to end?	3
Discretionary marks awarded for overall impression of the story's effectiveness.	3

Marking scheme for Letters

Technical Skills	Marks up to
Are the address and date placed correctly?	2
Appropriate salutation reflecting the type of letter and person addressed, e.g., Dear Sir/Madam etc.	2
How well does the letter show evidence of a suitable introduction/beginning, middle and end?	4
How well does the letter give a sense of completion?	5
Has the writer signed off the letter in a manner appropriate to the recipient, i.e., in a formal or informal manner?	2
How well has punctuation been used (including paragraphing)?	5
How accurate is the spelling?	5
Overall impression of presentation (neatness, legibility, correction of errors, etc.).	2
Content and Quality	**Marks up to**
How well does the letter reflect the requirements of the title given?	5
How well has the candidate covered the three areas suggested in the task advice?	9 (3 per area)
Is an attempt made to address the recipient using appropriate language, i.e., formal (standard English) or informal (non-standard English)?	3
How coherent is the letter, i.e., does it flow?	3
Discretionary marks for overall impression of the letter's effectiveness in achieving the task set.	3

For more detailed advice and practical help with understanding punctuation, punctuation for direct speech and layout for letter writing and reports, see *Tutor Master helps you Learn English – A Literacy Dictionary*.

© 2015 Tutor Master Services

Marking scheme for Speech Conversations

Technical Skills	Marks up to
Consistent use of capital letters to begin the words that are spoken.	3
Consistent use of speech marks (" ") to enclose words that are spoken.	3
Consistent use of final pair of speech marks to enclose other punctuation marks, e.g., full stops, exclamation and question marks	3
Consistent use of a new line used for each new speaker.	5
Consistent use of commas to separate words that are spoken from those unspoken.	4
How accurate is the spelling?	5
Overall impression of presentation (neatness, legibility, correction of errors, etc.).	2

Content and Quality	Marks up to
How well does the conversation reflect the requirements of the title given?	5
How coherent is the conversation, i.e., does it flow from beginning to end?	3
Does the conversation read/sound realistic?	2
How well does the conversation give a sense of completion?	3
How well have a variety of 'verbs of saying' been used by the speakers, e.g., said, replied, suggested, etc.?	5
How well have adverbs been used to convey the sense of expression of the speaker, e.g., replied happily, spoke sadly?	4
Discretionary marks for overall impression of the conversation's effectiveness in achieving the task set.	3

Marking scheme for Report

Technical Skills	Marks up to
How well does the report show evidence of a clear beginning, middle and end?	5
How well does the report give a sense of completion?	5
How well has punctuation been used (including paragraphing)?	5
How accurate is the spelling?	5
Overall impression of presentation (neatness, legibility, correction of errors, etc.).	2

Content and Quality	Marks up to
How well does the report reflect the requirements of the title given?	5
Is there evidence of originality of ideas that goes beyond reflecting the information set out in the reading passage?	5
How well has the candidate covered the three areas suggested in the task advice?	9 (3 per area)
How coherent is the report, i.e., does it flow from beginning to end?	5
Discretionary marks for overall impression of the report's effectiveness in achieving the task set.	4

Notes

© 2015 Tutor Master Services